Space Dinosaurs

By A.J. Gamboa

Illustrated by
Ernie Gamboa

COPYRIGHT © 2020
BY A.J. GAMBOA
ALL RIGHTS RESERVED

No part of this text may be reproduced, distributed, or transmitted in any form or by any means, including photocopying, recording, or other electronic or mechanical methods, or by any information storage and retrieval system without the prior written permission of the publisher, except in the case of very brief quotations embodied in critical reviews and certain other non commercial uses permitted by copyright law.

 For Baby Arlo

Some dino's went down in the dirt and got stuck.
They turned into fossils, it was very bad luck.

The rest were quite lucky and were gone with no trace. They were thrown through the sky and deep into space.

They survived the **BIG BANG** there were cheers and big roars! They would now call themselves the Space Dinosaurs!

The Space Dinosaurs love to play games and have fun they'll fly to each planet and start at the Sun.

It's much too hot to play near the Sun.
The Dino's make S'mores, then eat them and run.

They'll play marbles on Mercury with their best chum. The Dino's will play 'til they get a sore thumb.

Space Dino's go to Venus for a sweet getaway, and will stomp a love note on Valentine's Day.

They'll play Simon Says underneath the stars,
They'll play it all night on the red planet Mars.

They jump rope on Jupiter and sing songs in time.
The words aren't important as long as they rhyme.

When the Dino's hit Saturn they make time to stop.
The best deals can be found at the mall where they shop.

When the Dino's reach Uranus, it's really a trip!
They'll race around the planet in a fancy space ship.

By the time they reach Neptune
they're often quite tired.
The Dino's lay down, sleeping masks not required.

On the moon the Dino's will bring cheese to munch.
For breakfast, for dinner, and sometimes for lunch.

They think playing baseball near black holes is funny, but replacing all the lost balls can cost lots of money.

They'll play cards on a Comet if they so wish.
Then point and laugh as they yell...

They're freeze tag champions and have never once cheated. Against their alien friends they're still undefeated.

The Space Dino's will hide in an asteroid field, look closely for five and they'll all be revealed.

Next time you're up late and playing outdoors, scan the skies above for Space Dinosaurs!

WWW.SPACEDINOSAURBOOKS.COM

Made in United States
North Haven, CT
27 October 2023